Life Happens

10 Steps to Navigating Change & Transition

Life Happens
10 Steps to Navigating Change & Transition

by
Roberta Bogany

Copyright © 2021 by Roberta Bogany
All rights reserved. No part of this book may be reproduced, scanned,
or distributed in any printed or electronic form without permission.
First Edition: 2021
Printed in the United States of America
ISBN: 978-0-578-86503-4

To Jeffery and Destani: Without your support and encouragement, I would have never achieved this dream. Thank you for being you!

Acknowledgement

There are so many names that I could include here that have made an impact in my life over the years and made this book possible, but that within itself would be another book! So, I will keep it simple. My husband, Jeffery – Loving you and being loved by you is a gift. I am thankful to do life with you. My daughter Destani – I never thought that having a child would have brought change of the magnitude that I experienced as being your mother. Watching you grow lifted me. Watching you fly gave me wings. I love you puddin'! My family – you have seen me fall and get back up again. You have cheered me on and scolded me when necessary, and for that I will be eternally grateful. The tried-and-true friends (P, J, V, K, N) – you are the real MVPs! I will always love you for loving me unconditionally and for telling me the truth all of the time.

Although listed last, He is by no means the least – to God – for his continued hand of direction, guidance, grace, mercy, and love. You loved me first and always best.

Roberta Bogany

Life Happens: 10 Steps to Navigating Change & Transition

Introduction

When the first book was written in 2016, the mental and emotional space I was in from 2014-2016 was focused on creating a new life for myself after my daughter left for college. In doing that, I came to the realization that it wasn't that she had left that was the issue, it was the change to my world that had taken place. That was the empty nest – metaphorically. The nest was internal, and I recognized that the changes and transitions would empty me each time. Thus, the original title, Relining the Empty Nest.

Fast forward to 2021 –

So many changes! The daughter continues to live away and is growing and learning life lessons. I remarried in 2018 and that within itself has added changes and transitions to experience in aligning my life with my husband's and he with mine. 2020 brought to the world a pandemic, and we were forced to live life in a completely different way than we were accustomed. For me, I learned the beauty in slowing down – and I was grateful! I continued to work on the things I felt in my experience of growing older. I created a new normal and worked on achieving goals and dreams and becoming a better me. A fleeting thought of republishing. "Maybe," I said.

Over the past 5 years people who read the original book stated how glad they were that they did! They spoke of how the title misled the work within. They shared how the book had blessed them with its simplistic design yet the parts of myself that I had shared were real and honest. They also suggested that I publish it again with a new title. A classmate from junior high school really spoke to my heart with his words. "Maybe," I said.

For my birthday, this year I held a Virtual Craft Party for some friends – old and new. During the event people one of the attendees said that they wanted to take the time to tell me how my book had blessed them. They said that they had bought several copies to support but was excited to share it so others could benefit from it. They said how they felt I was speaking right to them. I was humbled and so very proud! She said I needed to republish. Those new friends who didn't know that I had written also wanted me to republish. "Maybe," I said.

Then my daughter called me and said that she had read my book. She told me how she had not read it when first published, but for whatever reason she woke up and picked it up – and she loved it! She told me that people needed the book during times like we are living in now. But here, let me allow her to share her words:

"I first read Relining the Empty Nest a few years after I received it. I was in a state of transition and had heard what the book had done for a few other women and felt it was time for me to read it. Because my mother was the author, it was a very intimate read. I learned things about my mother and felt like I could relate to her in a completely different way than I ever had. It humanized her further to me and gave me a different view of the mother I knew. I couldn't put it down. I finished the book (including the journaling prompts) in an hour or so and I felt a greater sense of understanding and compassion for both my mother and myself! Something I truly needed. I immediately thought about my group of friends who I talk to often and wanted to give them a

copy of the book. When I called my mother and she told me there were no copies left, I knew it was time to release it again. This book is easy to read, relatable, and spiritually uplifting! It's what the world needs right now with so many people going through their own versions of change and transition as a result of the 2020 pandemic, I know this book is a key to figuring out how to find your peace in the midst." - *Destani Smith*

After that – how could I NOT republish!

So here it is – the updated book. I gave it a new title and I have added some additional writings including some essays, thoughts, and social media notes. At the core, it remains what I hope in my heart to be something you can use to navigate the variations of change and transition you experience in your life. Go through the steps anytime you think you need to. I know that I do. Life Happens. Reline your internal nest and keep living!

Enjoy – and Be Blessed!

Bought Sense, Essays, & Random Thoughts

My mother, the one and only Exie Smith, used to say, "there is nothing like bought sense – the kind you have to pay for!" Of course, that sentence meant nothing to me until things in my life started to happen as I got older. Then I knew – it was the lessons you learned after the situation was over. Correction – it was the lessons you learned after the situation was over that you were warned not to get involved in in the first place! Yes, those lessons; and you know what? Those are the ones I am most grateful for. Those are the ones that have shaped and molded me. Those are the ones that I have shed the most tears over. Those are the ones that I have cried out to the Lord about. Those are the ones that I have eaten and shopped my way through! I'm sure that during some of those times God was saying "They/I/She/He/We told you, but you didn't want to listen." The truth is, I *was* listening, I just didn't think that what was being said applied to me. Isn't it funny that you will quickly hang on to things that you know don't apply to you but ignore the things that do?!? But I digress. This book is a collection of thoughts, stories, and learnings. Things that have happened to me in my life and random thoughts. It is my prayer that in sharing them they help someone else. Or at least let them see that their situation isn't the only one and you really do get past it and survive/thrive.

For those of you reading this that may not be Christian, it is not my intent to offend you, but I am a Christian and that part of my life is evident in some of these writings. Don't discount the lesson just because I use the word God or Jesus in it. Take what you can and use it!

These stories are real – they did happen to me and this is my viewpoint of them, which makes it my reality. Some of them are essays and some of them are me taking a stroll down memory lane. If in sharing I offend you or you think I'm talking about you, contact me, and let's talk about it. You may be right, or you may not. It may just be your conscience talking to you.

Finding Positive in the Negative

The Negative Thought: You Don't Matter

I was born in the 60's but I grew up in the 70's. The days of bell-bottom jeans and afros. 3 channels on 1 TV in the den that went off at midnight. Soul Train, Leave It to Beaver, and Mister Rogers Neighborhood. In my neighborhood in Houston, my house was on a corner across the street from my elementary school. This was the era of knowing your neighbors. Playing outside until it got dark. Drinking water out of the hose in the yard because Momma said, "Don't be running in and out of the house! You either stay in or out!" Riding your bikes around the neighborhood without fear of coming up missing. It was a time of being "in the moment" and having no worries. We went to school Monday through Friday, cleaned house Saturday morning, and played the rest of the day, the churched all day on Sunday. We were ok financially – at least that's what I thought. All I knew was that I didn't want for anything and had the same things that I saw advertised on TV. It wasn't until later that I found out that sometimes those things came from Goodwill. I'm not complaining, I'm a thrift store shopper even now. Those were the days.

I'm the youngest of 5 children and we are 5 years apart except the middle two who are a year apart. As the youngest, their version is that I got away with everything because I was the favorite. My version is by the time I came along my siblings had done everything already and my parents were just too tired to care – which was a good thing! Also because of the age difference, in my eyes, I grew up alone. We lived in a middle-class mixed neighborhood. I had Black and White friends. Usually, my Black friends didn't live close to me and so I only saw them on Sundays or if our mothers would take us to each other's house. I had some playmates in the neighborhood, but I was always different. They were White, I was Black. They were short, I was tall. They didn't wear glasses, and I did. They had long hair; my hair was short.

Their hair was straight, my hair was kinky. They were pretty –and in my eyes because it was not heard by my ears, I was not.

Bullying, as the term is used now, is not a new trend. I was bullied as a child not only by other children but sometimes by those close to me – primarily by my older brother who was closest to me in age and still living at home. Of course, during that time I was the pesky little sister to him, so he was only doing what some big brothers do. I know he didn't mean it – at least I do now, but at that time I wondered why he did not like me. Yes, I know what you are saying, "Children are cruel" and "Kids will be kids" and you're right to a certain extent, yet that does not remove the effect of it. Not only did I wonder why he did not like me, but I also wondered why no one in the house protected me, which in turn made me feel that no one loved me. No one told him what he was doing was wrong. This is where it begins, during childhood. This is the foundation of almost all issues or triumphs we will experience in life. What we learn as a child will haunt us, fuel us, or both.

Since I didn't hear the words cute, or pretty, or nice, or fun, I never thought that I was any of those things. I also thought that what I want, what I thought, how I felt, or what I needed just didn't matter. I was a part of the old school child rearing of not talking back and do as I say – period. I respected not only the position of authority in my household but the person who was in that position of authority. Plus, my Momma did NOT play! She disciplined us with a strong hand – and an even stronger belt! (Side note – my brother always said that she didn't get a switch off the tree like normal mothers, she pulled up the whole tree!) I was afraid of not only her wrath, but of her rejection. I wanted her to like me and to love me. I wanted to make her happy and it seemed that nothing I did, even making straight A's in school, accomplished that.

The Positive Lesson: You DO Matter

It took a long time, a really long time (I was in my late 30's) when I started to see that it wasn't so much how much I mattered to others, but how much I mattered to myself. See it's not always about the cheering and acknowledgement that you get from the outside. Don't get me wrong, it is nice to get it and everyone wants it from time to time, yet that should never be the only thing that will motivate you. Psalms 139:14 (New American Standard Bible, NASB) says, "I will praise you; for I am fearfully and wonderfully made: marvelous are your works; and that my soul knows right well."[1] Fearfully and wonderfully made! What? I get the "wonderfully" part, but what does the "fearfully" part mean? The Hebrew word for fearfully is "yare", pronounced "Yaw ray" meaning to revere or stand in awe of. With that being the case, and the second part of the verse says, "marvelous are your works", that means that God destined each of us to be a marvelous creation that is meant to be revered or respected. So, if that's what God intended, surely, we should be able to see that within ourselves. You DO matter!

SITUATIONS & LESSONS

My daughter has taught me more than she realizes. I learned from her to embrace my flaws. I learned to love my full lips and enhance the natural beauty that I couldn't see. I learned that I am stronger than I realize. I learned that being different is a good thing. I learned that not only am I a good mother, but I am also a fabulous woman overall!

Motherhood is the hardest job I have ever done, and the most rewarding. Another lesson was in the situation of becoming a single mother – it was never my desire to be in that club.

The Situation/Back Story

When I met Destani's father, I was living in New Jersey working at a college there as the bookstore manager. I worked for a management company and this was one of the stores that they managed. This was in the days of online chat rooms where you paid by the hour to be online. During my years with this company and traveling across the US, the online community had become where I hung out and felt a sense of belonging. No matter what city I found myself in they were always there and there was always someone online to talk to. Although social media has advanced by leaps and bounds and there are online relationships happening every day, during those years it made no sense to most people that you could be friends, close friends, with someone you never met.

When we began to have conversations outside of the chatroom, I told him that I was not interested in having a relationship with anyone. I had just come out of a bad relationship that had resulted in obtaining a restraining order and was just trying to get things back on track in my life. He said that was fine and I enjoyed conversations with him. I had home number, work number, and beeper number (yeah, I know) – and we would talk many times for hours that extended late into the night. He told me that he was divorced, and I believed him. I mean, why else would he give me all those phone numbers? When I called him at home, he answered. Surely, he couldn't be involved with anyone and be on the phone with me till the wee hours of the morning, right?

So, after 8 months of conversation, there was an offline event that was happening in Virginia. I decided to go, and he said he would meet me there and we go together. I took the train to Virginia the day before the party and he met me at the station. He took me to my hotel, and we had dinner that evening, and a few drinks. One thing led to another (blame it on the alcohol) and we had a one-time sexual encounter. Upon the realization that what happened had happened, I immediately sobered up!! "That shouldn't have happened," I said. He agreed and asked what happens next. We had a short discussion and ultimately, I told him that I couldn't handle anything outside of taking things one day at a time. He agreed. He left saying he would see me tomorrow for the party. Tomorrow never came. He never showed up. Didn't return calls. Wasn't online in the chat room. Nothing. Simply disappeared.

Upon my return to New Jersey, I convinced myself that he was probably as overwhelmed by what had happened as I was and to just give him some time. So, life went on and several weeks later I traveled to the annual manager's meeting for the company I was working for. Having dinner with some of the other female managers, I shared with them how strange I had been feeling lately. "You're pregnant," someone said, and we all laughed it off. Later that evening we were on the way to our hotel rooms and one of the ladies showed me that they had gone to a store and purchased a pregnancy test. "Ok, I'm game, I'll take it. It will be a hoot," I said.

I took the test and we sat outside of the bathroom door waiting the however many minutes for the test to be completed. This was the one where there would be a blue plus if you were pregnant and nothing if you were not. We all walked into the bathroom and counted to three to look. One…Two…Three…NEON BLUE PLUS

SIGN! There were a few seconds of silence following by this piercing wail! That wail came from me! WHAT? PREGNANT? This wasn't supposed to happen! We only had sex one time! (Hello, that's all it takes!) What am I going to do?

The rest of the meeting was a blur. I went back to New Jersey and tried to contact him. I also took several more pregnancy tests because that first one had to be defective! Finally, I went to the doctor. "Yeah, I know," I said, "I'm pregnant." More phone calls. He didn't respond. For two weeks I called and got no answer, no return calls, and I had no idea what I was going to do! I wasn't near family. I had made a couple of good friends, but I was basically still alone. Yes, I even thought about having an abortion. I didn't want to be a single mother. I was scared! I wanted to have a husband and then have children. Finally, I decided to call him and leave a message on his answering machine since he wasn't returning my calls.

The next day was to be the day I made the call. That morning I started spotting and went to the doctor. During the exam he asked me if I was going to keep the baby and I responded that I didn't know. He did an ultrasound and turned the screen to me to I could see. There was this little blurb on the screen that was blinking fast. "What is that?" I asked the doctor. "That's the baby's heartbeat," he responded. I started to cry. "You made a decision, didn't you?"

he said. "Yes," I responded, "I'm going to have this baby, it will be a girl, and her name will be Destiny." I changed the spelling when she was born.

When I got back to work that afternoon, I made the call and left the following message – "Hello, I've tried several times to contact you and since you won't return my calls, I will tell you what I have to say on your machine. I'm pregnant and you're the father." Within two hours he called back. "You can't have that baby," he said "Children shouldn't be conceived like this. You just didn't play the game right!" (GAME?!?!?!) Then the real kicker! "My wife heard that message..." "YOUR WHO?" I yelled. "Yes," he responded, "You knew that I was married" MARRIED?!?! "No", I said "I would have remembered that little tidbit of information!" I told him that he needed to get over it. I was pregnant and he was the father. I told him that he lied; I didn't...so he would just have to deal with it.

When I hung up, I sat and thought, how could I have been so stupid? Why didn't I know? But he didn't do anything that gave an indication of being married.

The Lessons

Part 1 – All things really do work together for good! When I think about the timing of that conversation, I realize that there was a bigger plan in place. If he had called me at any point before that doctor's appointment, he may have been able to convince me to not have the baby. Yet it did not happen until I had spoken the words of confirmation that I was going to have the baby and naming her!

Part 2 - If the intent of a person is to be deceptive and manipulative, then they will go as far as they need to in order to carry it out. It's NOT your fault! It is who they are. So, don't spend a lot of time beating yourself up about what happened. It's natural to feel betrayed, hurt, and angry. Feel what you feel and work on moving forward. This man decided that my statement of just wanting to be friends was a challenge to him. I became something he needed to conquer. It was a game to him. It took me a long time to realize this lesson. I carried the guilt about her conception for many years. Yet she is the best thing to happen to me. Truly the wind beneath my wings. She is beautiful, smart, and talented, and I am honored to be her Mother.

The Situation/ Lessons Combo– Insecurity

There have been various times, that I have revealed to people that I am insecure, and their immediate response is that I never would have thought that bout you. "You're so outgoing, you're so funny, you're such a people person." Those responses made me wonder. Firstly, what is it about me that they can see that I can't?

Secondly, why can't I believe those same things about myself. What is at the core of why I feel that I am insecure? What is it that I am comparing myself against? What is it that is causing me to think negatively about who I am? If you're really, really honest with yourself in the examination of what's at the core of all those things you will realize that it started long before now. Sometimes it goes back to childhood. Children are just as afraid of what's different about the people that they come in contact with as adults are which is why we have racism, discrimination, and all those other things. Most of the time it's simply that those persons are afraid of someone who is different from them.

One item for me was my height. As a child, being very tall, other kids made fun of me. I didn't realize that some were afraid of me. Little did they know that I was afraid of them – so we just ran around being scared of each other. Their fear of me was shown in aggression. My fear of them was shown in retreat.

The more I retreated the more I tried to find an outlet for myself that was not confrontational, not intimidating. Something that was safe. I needed something that was not going to lash back at me and make me feel bad about who I was. Most of the time I found that safety in music, movies, and books. Particularly books because I could become the character in the book that had the most fun or was the prettiest or who was the heroine of the story. My escape into books in my mind let me see how different life could be. But it was a distorted view because it showed me a world of fantasy. A world that someone had created – it wasn't real. I started to think that relationships and families were what I read about in books and saw on TV. I started to think that I was going to be Annette Funicello and Frankie Avalon was going to find me on the beach and he was going to pursue me, and we were going to twist the night away beach blanket bingo and he would kiss me, and all would be forever ok. I would imagine that Elvis Presley was going to sing me a song on his guitar and tell me that he was going to love me tender and that would be the end of it. Yes, my knights in shining armor were white men from the movies. That was all that I saw that represented itself in a way of speaking and showing love.

Along with the distorted view of families and relationships, it also created a distorted view of men. My father was very quiet. My mother was the disciplinarian and the voice of the family. My Dad was not Mike from the Brady Bunch, so I wondered why didn't my Dad love me? He never said he loved me never said he cared. He was not a person of expression which I now understand, but as a child all I wanted was to be loved and held and to be told that I was loved and that I was ok just the way that I was and that didn't happen in my family. For me having the personality that I have it has been hard for me to remove myself from that situation and get past it. That's been something that I've worked on for the last 20 plus years and still working on it. I know you're thinking, just get over it – but think about it. Every day that I felt the way that I did added a layer. Just like yo feet, (yes, I said "yo") the longer you go without taking care of them and getting that pedicure, the thicker and harder that skin builds up. It's the same with insecurities and negative thought processes.

There are some people who have the ability to shake things off very easily. There are some people who have the ability to remove themselves from a situation and "get over it" – even though sometimes they may say they have gotten over it, but they have only internalized it and are hiding from the reality of how they feel, who they are, and what has happened in their life. Hiding from the reality still does not allow you to heal from the situation. What it does is cause the pain to manifest itself in other ways – drug addiction, alcoholism, gambling, craving attention, sexual promiscuity, isolation, and sometimes you just become downright mean! That begins the cycle of "They hurt me so I'm going to hurt someone else", or not fully giving of yourself in relationships to protect yourself, and so on, and so on.

My path to overcoming the insecurity is one that I am continuing. I still have my moments of feeling inadequate. Ironically, during the time that I was dealing with the Empty Nest

Syndrome after my daughter went away to college, I really dug deep into these feelings and started to peel them away and reveal the good in myself. I had become very cynical about everyone and everything because I thought that life had dealt me a bad hand and I was hurting. Now mind you, I had a good job, a vehicle, I wasn't missing meals and there was a closet full of clothes. Yet there was still a void because I was missing love. Not just relational love but self-love.

The Situation – Divorce

My first husband and I had not been happy through a lot of our marriage, yet I wasn't sure of all the reasons why. We didn't communicate well so I spent a lot of time trying to figure out the answer to questions that only he could answer. I finally came to the realization that our marriage would not work and had set a time frame to talk with him about it. Before that time arrived, I was scheduled to attend a conference for work that required me to be away for a week. I wanted to see if during this time away that we could connect. You know, absence making the heart grow fonder and all of that. While I was away, we talked daily. Sometime three or four times a day and honestly, I was encouraged by it. He told me that he had taken Destani to spend some time with my mother. This wasn't unusual so I thought nothing of it. The day I returned, I got off of the plane and he was not there to greet me. I called. Twice. No answer.

He called me back and told me that I needed to call my mother or someone to come and pick me up because he was in New Orleans. His mother had been sick and any other time I would have asked if she was ok, but this time I knew it was different. "You're not coming back are you," I said. "No," he said, and hung up. Stunned, I placed a couple of calls and got someone to come and pick me up. When I arrived at home, I went into the front door and thought, hmm, nothing is different. My friend had stayed outside. She said she would wait. My mother was on the way. I walked down the hall and turned into the bedroom. My clothes and personal items from the dresser and nightstand were on the floor and all of the bedroom furniture was gone. I walked through the living room and through the kitchen to go into the garage. The entire garage was empty. Bare. For the 5 years of our marriage, we had accumulated things and placed them here. A few months prior we had purchased some new items and placed the old ones in the garage. All were gone. He had packed up everything and moved out. I opened the garage door to the outside and my friend, my mother and Destani stood there. We all just looked at each other.

For a moment I didn't do or say anything, but that silence was interrupted by a few choice words from my mother. She followed me into the house and continued to give her opinion about what had transpired. After she had seen the bedroom, I asked her to take Destani home with her for the night. She did so and my friend left.

I walked back into the house and went back into the bedroom. I couldn't believe how he had just thrown my things on the floor. I called him and he answered. I asked why and he said there was no reason to go into all of that. I told him I wasn't angry that he left, I was angry at how he did it. No response. I hung up. I sank against the wall and slid to the floor as I let the tears fall. I cried for about an hour then thought, "Ok, I have some things to do." I picked up a pad and pen and started to make a list. I called a couple of male friends from church and they came by to change the locks on the doors. I'm not sure if I was numb but I know I was in work mode. I had a child to raise and a life to live – time to get started on it.

This happened in October. The next day I began to make calls and get things switched to my name. It was a cold day and that evening I couldn't get the house warm. I called the same friend from church and he came by to check the pilot light on the hot water heater in the attic. "It won't light," he said. I called the gas company and found out he had turned off the gas. Turned. It. Off. Without a word and me with a child in the house. I was furious! I set up service to be restored but of course it wouldn't be that evening. I called him and his response was he did it because it was in his name. I told him he could have given me a chance to get things done. I couldn't believe that he thought I would leave things in his name. I guess when you do dirt you expect dirt back. We spent the night at my mother's house.

Over the next few days/weeks I went about the business of removing him from our lives. I filed for divorce. I read my bible. I cried some. I cursed some. Overall, honestly, I was relieved. Not long after he left, Destani asked why he didn't love us anymore. I told her I didn't know why and that we had done nothing wrong. See, this was the only "Daddy" that she knew. Now he, just like her father, had abandoned her. I contacted him and asked him to call Destani to let her know that she didn't do anything and that none of this was her fault. He said he would, but the call never came. I believe that this has had an impact in her life more than either of us realized it would. I continue to pray that she recognizes that the actions and issues are theirs, not hers.

About a month after we were divorced, he contacted me to ask me to keep him on my insurance and in return he would pay my cell phone bill (insert blank stare). I told him that being on my insurance was a benefit of being my husband. He was no longer my husband, so he no longer received benefits. Period.

I too felt abandoned, but also relieved. I wanted to know why because I wanted to know what I needed to do on my part to be better for the next relationship. After a while it wasn't that important to know why anymore. It just was. Accept it and move on. The reality of that helped to bolster me in some ways but I still had a little "what did I do" in my mind.

About 6 months after we divorced, he called me to ask if he could come by. I asked why. He said he wanted to come by to discuss reconciling (Insert confused stare followed by "have you lost your mind" look at the phone). I asked, "Why would you want to go back to someone who doesn't know why you left in the first place? What do you think is different? What behavior do you think has changed?" He said we didn't need to discuss all of that. I said we did. He said if we discussed it and it wasn't going to end with reconciling then he didn't want to do it. I told him there would be no reconciliation for the following reasons:

    I did not love him,

    I did not like him,

    I did not trust him,

    and I did not respect him.

I hung up.

The Lesson

    Know your worth – and demand it.

SOCIAL MEDIA DATED ESSAYS

The following essays were originally posted as notes on social media.

2009 - No More Disclaimers

A friend of mine who read my "Lies like a Rug" post called me up and said that I shouldn't have posted the disclaimer. She said that my words stood on their own merit, and that I had initially stated that they were my "personal observations, opinions, and sometimes random incoherent rants" so no need to do that.

That started me to thinking – (yes, I know how dangerous that is, but I can't help myself.) I wondered, why it is that so many of us will give a disclaimer to something that we think, do, or feel? Hmm…

Disclaimer is defined as "the act of disclaiming; the renouncing, repudiating, or denying of a claim. a statement, document, or assertion that disclaims responsibility, affiliation, etc.;"[2] Upon consideration of that definition, I would say that most of the time, we do not want to renounce or deny what we have stated, but more so to further explain our rationale for our statements or actions. In pondering this further, I thought that we could use some alternative words or phrases:

1. **Cause** – I said what I said CAUSE that is what I wanted to say!
2. **Reason** – If folk wouldn't act the way they act, then I wouldn't have REASON to act like I act!
3. **Delimitating factors** – We won't even go there.
4. **Alibi** – Only necessary in situations that could ultimately end up in facing parents, spouses, significant others, the police, or on Judge Mathis!
5. **"See what had happened was…."** - You already know that what will follow that phrase is a lie added to the lie that started the conversation in the first place!

Legally, disclaimers keep a lot of companies off of the hot seat, but in interpersonal relationships, it's just best to choose something a little different. Now you have a few more options!

2010 - Let's LOVE!

February…the month of love. As a single woman this can be a stressful month! My brothers, you are not the only ones who can sometimes dread this time of year! You know the drill; some single men avoid getting involved with anyone in February and December so they will not have to deal with the holiday stuff. Or if you are involved, you are not sure what kind of gift to give. What is too much? What is not enough? Now I admit, I am a sentimental one, so most holidays are on my "to do" list, but I have learned over the years that it is more important to have the right perspective when it comes to February and the "V" word - Valentine's Day.

My perspective on this has changed significantly twice, well three times now that I really think about it, during my 40+ years. The first time was after my daughter was born, and I made the decision that I wanted her to understand that Valentine's Day was not just for lovers, but also for those that you love. I wanted her to know that you do not have to have a man in your life to enjoy the holiday. As a result, we have gone out to dinner, movies, and exploring. I have bought her special trinkets and gifts, and even just made sure she had a card to commemorate the day. The second change was during my marriage. Even though during our courtship we had extended conversation about our likes, our dislikes, and our expectations, my now Ex-husband seemed to always forget that it was Valentine's Day. And he worked retail, but that is an entirely new discussion. Don't get me wrong, I was not one of those women that expected roses and candy and expensive gifts - a card would have been nice; just something to let me know that he remembered me on that day. Now I also believe that this is one of those things that society has helped us to distort our view of. Think about it, the Halloween candy has not been marked down before you begin to see Christmas decorations on display in the stores! The day after

Christmas, the Valentine's Day promotions start popping up. We are bombarded with what we should do for this day. I can hear the music now...listen..."every kiss begins with K"...sigh.

The third, and in my opinion, the most important change, happened last year. Valentine's Day 2009 was the first time in a few years that I was alone on Valentine's Day. Weeks before the day I thought about what I could do to make it a good day for myself. I had already put together something for Destani, so that was taken care of, but what about me?

Was that a selfish thought? Or just proactive thinking? Well, in order to decide what the day would look like I had to first be honest with myself as to where I was at that point. I was newly divorced. I was single - again. Was I bitter, no, not really. I was glad that the situation had finally come to a resolution. I had no regrets about anything and wished him well. I had successfully made it through Christmas, New Year's, and my birthday, so I was doing well so far. But *this* day....this was *the* day for us who are romantic at heart (I am), for those who are sentimental (I am), and for those who enjoy loving and being loved (Yes, I do). My church family was busy preparing for the married couples' event, so I couldn't be a part of that. I was too old for the teen dance and too young for the senior citizens event. What would I do? Who do I love?

I made a list of things I thought I would enjoy whether it was

Valentine's Day or not. Those things are What I love. What is it that makes you smile just to think about it? What is it that makes you anxious for the day to arrive so you can experience it? What is it that you truly enjoy but may not get a lot of opportunity to do? Those are your list of What's.

My list was short. I just could not shake the reminders of the day being *that* day! So, I stopped trying to forget it. I began to ruminate on it a little. I thought about all the ways that I had been disappointed on that day. I thought of all of the tears I had shed as a result of allowing myself to feel "less than" on that day because no one sent me flowers, or a card, or bought me candy when I was single. I thought of how unloved I felt because my husband had forgotten me on that day. I thought of all the commercials and movies that add to the ideology that we place on "that" day. I decided to give new meaning to that day no matter what my relationship status dictated. I would do the only thing I could think of - I would spend the day loving me. Why not? After all, that is who I love! I. Love. ME!

I made it a point to be "away" that weekend. I told my family that I would be out of town. Not that I was hiding from anyone; well, I *was* hiding from my daughter, but that was because I knew she would be concerned about me and I was not 100% sure that I would make it through that weekend without some tears. So, I became "away". I looked at my list and chose a couple of things. I got up early and stayed out all day. I had breakfast - alone, in a place I had not been before. I shopped. I tried on clothing that I had not had the nerve to try before. I had lunch in a popular spot that I knew would be full of people, but I did something different at lunch. I chose to sit in the bar area, not at a table in the back corner. Guess what happened? I had a great time! I focused on enjoying the place and those who were there without focusing on the day! I met a few people. We talked and shared! After lunch I went to the movies, alone, and saw something that I wanted to see without worrying if someone else would object to it. I did a little more shopping, then I went to dinner and followed the same formula that I had used for lunch. I had more fun! By the time I got home, I was exhausted. I took a long bath, had a glass of wine while reading, and went to bed. On Sunday, I got up, went to church and had much to praise God for! I had overcome a huge obstacle for myself! I had learned a new way to Love. - a new How!

It is easy for us to define the Who and What of Love, but How do you love? Do you only look to be given love or do you give love to others? The gospel group Commissioned sang a song in the late '80's that said, "Love isn't love 'till you've given it away."[3] WOW! That is powerful! Love is not just an emotion; it is an action word. You must do it so it can be seen along with being felt. 1

Corinthians 13:4 (NASB) says, "Love is patient, love is kind and is not jealous; love does not brag and is not arrogant." [1] So while all of those are emotions, things you feel, we know that there are actions that take place as a result of those emotions. Can't you remember a time when someone said to you, "I love you," and your response to them was, "Show me."

So How are you showing love? Is there something that makes your children say, "I just love when Mom/Dad does _____!" Do you treat your customers in a way that makes them tell their friends, "I give them my business because I love how they treat me!" Can your friends and family pinpoint something and say, " I love how he or she _____."

Think on it like this song[4]:

If I can help somebody as I pass along
If I can cheer somebody with a word or song
If I can show somebody he is traveling wrong,
Then my living (and loving) shall not be in vain.

I am looking forward to this Valentine's Day to see what will happen since I've learned a new How! Let's LOVE!

L - Look at the who, what ,and how you love

O - Sometimes the best gifts are OUTSIDE the box!

V - Valentine's Day should be a constant!

E - Let love shine through your actions EVERYDAY!!

2010 - Extreme Makeover

While on a cruise recently, I was in my cabin watching the show Extreme Makeover. You know how it works - the foundation of the show is based on a person or families who have a situation in their life which prevents them from being able to live in a "suitable" home. The Extreme Makeover team comes in and builds the family a new home to help their life improve. In a sense, they change the external to work to improve the internal. I wondered how many of us realize that we should each experience our own extreme makeover – but from the inside out!

I met a young man who is embarking on a new path in his life. He has a passion for sports and a heart for children – and is trying to combine those two. He originally was not considering starting a business, but the more he shared with me the more I could see his vision become a new business. He had been laid off and not having success in finding another job and I told him that perhaps this is why. I saw a light in his eyes when he would begin to talk about working with those kids and what he wanted to do to make an impact in their lives. I shared with him some foundational knowledge that I had as a previous business owner and a corporate administrator. He then began to talk about his image and the difficult time he is having in changing the way he dresses, speaks, and those he associates with. Not that his "associates" are the wrong ones, just on a different level. He doesn't want to disrespect his friends but has a sincere desire to be a better man – both spiritually and mentally. I told him that I could see God at work in his life.

I also shared with him that sometimes we must have two different personalities – a professional side and a personal side – and there is nothing wrong with it! The key is to discover how to balance the two so that there isn't a situation that could be "discovered" that would destroy either side. I shared with him that sometimes, it takes one individual to have the courage to be begin the change process for others to follow suite. "Don't follow the trend," I said to him, "set the trend!"

It's so important to recognize that who you are as a person – be it a business owner, professional, or just as an "ordinary Joe" is so much more than what you present on the outside. It's who you are inside and 'that' comes shining through. Consider this statement "You can take the person out of the country, but you can't take the country out of the person." Why is that? It is because "country" is who that person is on the inside. It shines through not matter what type of clothing you wear or what type of car you drive. There is a "still small voice" that whispers to you when you know that you are at a point to elevate yourself from your current situation.

2009 was a year of change for me - marital status, financial, career – and my initial fear was how I was going to "look" to others in this new start, and as a result, I tried to reinvent myself – externally – with some positive and some negative results. As God continues to work on me, I began to understand that it was not my external but some internal changes that were in order. Not that I am a horrible person, but a few of the things that were hindering my elevation to who HE would have me to be in order to become complete in HIM were the things that I was trying to keep from happening on the inside. When I started to allow the internal to change, the external changes caused people to say "What has happened to you? You have this glow!"

My friend, Tony Haynes, wrote a poem called, "Live As If You Have Arrived"[5]

Live as if…

Y ou have arrived to that place

O f revelation

U nforgettably described as destiny & destination

A lthough still on your journey to a

R ainbow pre-archived

E very sign tells you…

…To live as if you have arrived

I n the flesh to that space called Soul Salvation

N irvana for a passenger who purposefully passes…

T hrough the portal of presumption to

H ail the proclamation that

E vokes power & persuasion to the masses

D ive in wholeheartedly

R evel in your parted sea

I n a way that channels Moses once you've dived

V ersus Pharaoh and his army be

E xcursion ready

R eadily

S et to live your life as if you have arrived

S o those with trepidation

E xit from their station

A rmed with a sense of hope in overdrive

T o wander less and from this day …

As you do - so will they

Believe before they leave they have arrived.

When you go through an internal makeover, you begin to live as if you have arrived. You begin to walk in your destiny and feel the power that has been in you all along. YOU ARE IN THE DRIVERS SEAT – but God has the best GPS system available! Let 2010 be the year of your Extreme Makeover!

2011 - As a Man Thinketh

A few months ago, a Pastor was preaching a series called "The Aroma of Praise" (Psalm 112: 1-9) and he said, "praise replaces pity!" That resonated with me and I began to consider how many times that I had resorted to being the Queen of the Pity Party instead of praising God in advance for what I knew he was going to do in my life.

I printed that phrase out and placed it in several different places. One of them being the computer monitor on my desk at work. During those days when my coworkers were really getting on my nerves I would look over and see that phrase and immediately rethink my response to the situation. "Look Roberta," I said to myself, "there is going to be somebody who gets on your nerves no matter where you work! Stop allowing that one person to completely alter the view of your job here. You like what you do, focus on that!"

So, I began to bring more to the forefront the things that I enjoyed about my job and people noticed that I wasn't complaining anymore. "Have things gotten better with that person," they would ask. My response was "No, but I don't focus on that. I let them be themselves and I keep on moving." As a result, my response to things changed. More of Him, less of ME.

After this past weekend at a women's conference that provided CLARITY, COMFORT, and CONFIRMATION, I knew that I was ready for whatever purpose that God had been preparing me for in the past few years.

When we battle the enemy in the way that we can – not allowing him to distract, discourage, and dissuade us from doing what we know we can and should be doing, then we open the door for God to come in and do all that we can't.

I am an entirely different person in God…and I am going to act like it!

2013 - I AM Michelle Obama!

Over the past few years since the Obama's have come into the spotlight, I have heard many men say, "I want me a Michelle Obama". That statement has increased many times over after her outstanding speech last night during Day 1 of the Democratic National Convention. Well fellas, we are here! Yes, I said WE! We are the women who support our men – we encourage him. We pray with him and over him. We "hold it down" when life beats him up, and we love him with all that is within us. We take good care of our families no matter what the economy provides, and we make sure that there is balance – fun, discipline, and God. We are intelligent and beautiful. We are strong and emotional. We are concerned about our communities and our bodies. We are enlightened and entertaining. We are sophisticated and classy. We are women of Faith. We speak eloquently and don't have to announce our arrival – people know we are there. We are elegant and we carry ourselves like ladies. We are also many times overlooked.

We are sometimes darker than Rihanna. Our hair doesn't always flow like Beyoncé's. Our breasts are full or just relatively "normal" and we don't let them spill over everything that we wear like some of the latest reality stars. Our clothes are stylish and fit without cutting off our circulation. We may not have booties like Nikki Minaj. Yet nonetheless, in the perfection of the way that God has created us, we are fine – make that foine! So, in the same vein of the statements made after the tragedy in Florida, I stand and proclaim, I AM Michelle Obama….where are YOU, Barack?

2002/2009 - The Other Side of Through

Bought sense. That's what my Mother always called it. It was what you gain after you had experienced something. It was the lesson you carried with you from that day forward. As a Christian, it is the wisdom of God springing forth out of a difficult situation. It is where you land when you arrive on the other side of through. You know what "through" is, right? It's when you've cried all night long, or you are in a situation that you have no solution to, or when you just can't seem to pull yourself up out of that depression that you're in and people ask you, "What is wrong?" and you can only reply "I'm just going through". James Bignon has a song that reminds us "there's a blessing on the other side of through."[6]

I recently was reflecting on the number of "throughs" that I have survived and also in the deliverance received in the series of messages by a pastor during a sermon on "It's My Time". Is it really my time, I asked myself? Is it my season? In arriving on the other side of my latest "through", God revealed to me the essence of what "your time and season" really is.

The 4 seasons or nature's cycle are all something that we are familiar with, and each season takes approximately 3 months to complete itself. So, when we hear the words "it's your season or it's your time", we immediately think that our prayers will be answered instantaneously, or at least by the end of the next season. We begin to rejoice! In 3 months, everything will be alright! But wait, we are still on God's time, not our time, and the amount of time that is necessary for us to complete our season or our cycle is completely dependent upon where we are in our walk with God. There are different elements of your season just as there are different elements of each season of nature. Recognizing that you need God's guidance in your life is one element. Growing in your knowledge of the word is another element. Recognizing that Momma's relationship with God is not yours is another element. Examining where you are in your personal relationships and removing the toxic people from your surroundings is another element.

A few weeks ago, someone emailed me a list of statements that I sat down and compared it to the bits of wisdom that God has given to me in arriving at the other side of through. I will share some of these with you.

1. "When you want something you've never had, you've got to do something you've never done." – Thomas Jefferson. A college degree was something that I never thought I would achieve. There was always an "if only" standing between the degree and myself. One day, I decided that I would find a program that would allow me to work, be a good mother, and obtain my degree. I didn't know how I would pay for it or even if I would qualify for financial aid. That was in October of 1999. I began at LeTourneau University in January of 2000 and I will graduate this December with a degree in Business Management. Never say never.

2. **"What you are willing to move away from determines what God will bring to you."** Another sermon shared about running to meet our giants. My giant is insecurity. I stand witness to you today that every time I face that insecurity head on, God allows me to achieve my goal. I always felt that I was too tall, too large, too dark, hair too short, etc. to do anything that was associated with "beauty". Last year, I faced that giant of insecurity and entered the Miss American Achievement pageant. I won the city title, state title, and ultimately became first runner up for the national title. I moved away from fear, and God brought me accomplishment.

3. **"God never consults your past to determine your future."** There are things in my past that I am not proud of, just as there are in yours. If I continued to keep my head down because of the things that I had not been able to do in the past, I wouldn't have seen the doors and windows opening to me for the new improved and exciting blessings that God has lay before me now and in the future. This too shall pass - let it go. God has prepared us and is preparing us for exactly where we need to be in his kingdom, and he

knows what he has brought us through to get there.

4. "The only difference between your present and your future is your wisdom." My personal relationships have left a lot to be desired, and as a result, I remain a single woman – but I tell you, I would rather wait for the **best** man that God is preparing for me than settle for the **good** man that I **think** I need. Stand still and know that with God **ALL** things are possible.

We all make mistakes and will continue to do so. Just remember that the joy is in knowing that with each mistake, there is wisdom to be gained and a step to be made. With each step you get closer to the desires of your heart and the riches that God has prepared just for you. Don't be discouraged by the storms that come your way, just know that 'through" is something that we all experience. You have either been through, are going through, or are about to go through – but know that there is a blessing, and added wisdom in the elements of your season, on the other side of through.

THEN AND NOW....2009

This was written 7 years ago, and yes, I still go through, and I still reflect on these aspects of what God is trying to show me as a result of whatever it is that I am going through. I did get my bachelor's degree; I also completed my master's degree in Education in 2006 and am working on my PhD. I got married to a man that I thought was the man for me – he was a **good** man, but not the **best** man that God has for me - and now I am divorced. I continue to strive for the prize that is awaiting me at the end of each lesson. I continue to examine who and what is in my life and whether or not it should remain there, and I tell you, **every time** that I **remove** some garbage from my life **God showers me with goodness!** I am not as insecure as I used to be. Do I question things – yes, sometimes, but don't get it twisted, I am fabulous! I am a **beautiful** woman with a huge heart and a loving spirit – and **nothing** you do will take that away from me! It **is** who God created me to be – and the **fake** in you cannot remove the **real** in me!

Now with these thoughts in mind, **why** wouldn't you look **forward** to the **other side of through?**

2009 - 40 Things I've Come to Realize

1. I've come to realize that I am an awesome woman of God although it may not be as you define it.

2. I've come to realize that men will do exactly what they want to do...PERIOD....even though I may not like it.

3. I've come to realize that it's important to stay connected with real friends – don't let life keep you from it.

4. I've come to realize that overall, I AM a fabulous woman – smart, sexy, and strong!

5. I've come to realize that sex is much better when you're not preoccupied with the thought of catching some dreadful disease.

6. I've come to realize that turning 40 is freeing….and I'm getting better as I get older.

7. I've come to realize that you really don't appreciate the lessons you parents taught you until you become an adult.

8. I've come to realize that God has given me many talents – and I don't utilize them out of fear.

9. I've come to realize that I although not technically a morning person, I enjoy quiet mornings with God and a cup of coffee.

10. I've come to realize that I am not working in a role is the best for me…and I need to take action to change that.

11. I've come to realize that the man who gets me will be a lucky man.

12. I've come to realize that life is good!

13. I've come to realize that I need a circle of strong positive people around me…and that's ok.

14. I've come to realize that I still have some work to do on my insecurities and fears.

15. I've come to realize that there is nothing wrong with enjoying learning new things – I'm a Geek!

16. I've come to realize that Facebook has been a great tool for many things!

17. I've come to realize that family is very important to me and that won't change.

18. I've come to realize that I will stop apologizing for what I want out of life – I deserve it!

19. I've come to realize that I am good at helping others find their niche.

20. I've come to realize that dating a man who is the same height as I am, is not too bad!

21. I've come to realize that you are height makes a difference in how your clothes do fit.

22. I've come to realize that what is considered freaky for some may be normal for others.

23. I've come to realize that my daughter is smart, talented, and beautiful.

24. I've come to realize that I should record a CD – if only for myself.

25. I've come to realize that my Mother loves me even though I could choke her sometimes!

26. I've come to realize that I have no regrets from my marriage and no regrets in being divorced.

27. I've come to realize that negative people drain my energy, and I won't allow it.

28. I've come to realize that my personality is a good thing – even if

just for me!

29. I've come to realize that I have to learn to relax and allow what will be to come to pass.

30. I've come to realize that I have to have some type of interaction with people in order to energize.

31. I've come to realize that I am blessed with wonderful friends!! I LOVE YOU GUYS!!

32. I've come to realize that big breasts are overrated!

33. I've come to realize that I am destined to lead in some capacity.

34. I've come to realize that I have the power to create most any situation that I desire.

35. I've come to realize that I don't use that power nearly enough.

36. I've come to realize that the people I've been intimidated by were actually afraid of me all along.

37. I've come to realize that it does not make me less than a woman to not be Suzy Homemaker.

38. I've come to realize that some people with a WHOLE lot of money are generally miserable, but I'll test that theory for research purposes.

39. I've come to realize that all things really DO work together for good!

40. I've come to realize that it is possible to meet great friends online!

Random Thoughts – Just for Fun

- How do you know if buttermilk is bad? I mean, it's buttermilk!
- Did chivalry and common courtesy die together? Was it a murder-suicide?
- Is there a timer on bananas that starts as soon as you purchase them? #greentodaybrowntomorrow
- Evolution/change/transition....aren't they all a component of growth? You can't grow without evolving and you can't evolve without changing and you can't change without transitioning to another place; another level; a different mindset. Being stagnant is not good and not God. It's all about hope.
- Don't get so caught up on what's on the outside, that you miss a real jewel of a man or woman on the inside. #dismissthesuperficialstuff
- Hmmm, is it wrong to be mad if someone sends you message with a LOT of spelling errors?
- Why do you turn the radio down when you are LOOKING for an address? Does it make you see better? SMH...
- If you wouldn't let a day go by without talking to or spending time with your special someone/significant other, shouldn't the same go for God?
- Why are we so quick to dismiss someone because of their MINOR shortcomings when they are accepting of our MAJOR ones? IJS...

Disrespect during a discussion is not a discussion - it's just disrespect...IJS...

I see a lot of posts and hear conversations from guys about not being able to find a "good woman". Do you really know what to do when you find one? IJS...

Why do folks wear black to outdoor events and it's 743 degrees outside?

I'm sorry, but I can't attend a church where the pastors last name is "dollar"! #yallknowyouthoughaboutit

If someone shares with you info about a struggle, PLEASE don't say "Oh that's easy!" Something that comes easily to you may not for them - and to say that makes them feel even more defeated than they already feel. #showcompassion #standintheirshoes

You gotta keep doing what you did to get you there, after you get there...and sometimes you gotta do a little MORE!

Why is it when you finally start to do what you've been afraid to do, you're no longer afraid, just knee-knocking nervous?

Pinky rings on men...why?

If you ask me what I think or feel and I tell you, do NOT then tell me that is NOT what I think or feel. You are not me – you cannot speak for me.

I love it when I sit on a deep sofa and my feet don't touch the floor! #tallgirl

- If Hummus is " dip made from cooked, mashed chickpeas, or other beans, blended with tahini, olive oil, lemon juice, salt and garlic", why not just call it "bean dip"? #fancyname #ilikebeandipwithfritos #fritosarenothealthy #tahiniisgroundupsesameseeds
- I'd like to see women go back to wearing "maternity" clothes instead of stuff that looks too little.
- The older I get, the more I like naps!
- I wonder what happened to the Chocolate Factory after Charlie got it from Willy Wonka?
- Why do folks wear black to outdoor events and it's 743 degrees outside?

    ...and now back to business!

- It's all about CHANGE AND TRANSITION

- It's a choice. I choose to learn, grow, and become better. I choose to be positive, loving, compassionate, supportive, and kind. I choose to continue to have dreams, goals, and aspirations - and do the work to make them happen. I choose change - create. hope, avoid negativity, growing, every day. #theonlythingconstantischange

- Change isn't comfortable, and sometimes you have to fall a couple of times before you get it right, but in spite of the fear, I still move forward...a small step at a time...and that's a good thing! Take my hand and help me walk - that's what friends do!

It's when you seriously make a change (it really is a lifestyle) in how you do things; whether it's how and what you eat, your clothing, friends, or thought processes, those old habits just aren't appealing anymore! Even if you slip, that still small voice keeps you from traveling too far down that slippery slope and causes you to not dwell on it - shake it off and keep pushing forward to the next "it" #gotit #didit #lostit #completedit #ranit #liftedit #wearingit #lovingit #digginit

"**The Only Constant** in Life Is **Change**." ~ Heraclitus

Preface

"Just when the Caterpillar thought the world was over, it became a Butterfly"
— *English Proverb.*

This book is not just for those who are empty nesters in the traditional sense. For some of you, your children may still be at home but are in high school. Some of you may not have children at all but have been married and are now divorced or widowed. Some of you may find yourself newly retired or as has been the situation for many in the past decade or so, been laid off or had your company to close. This book is for all of us whose lives have been spent in giving of ourselves to others or placed the focus on other things, but now have to figure out what life looks like for us after life happens.

I did not want this to be a deep intense book but an easy read that would provide some simple steps along with sharing some of the story of my own journey. (Plus, I'm over 50, I use big letters!) Please use the journaling pages at the end of each step to record your thoughts and feelings as you go through the process reflecting on how life has happened to you and of lining your own empty nest. You will be glad you did when you revisit this book just to see the growth you have made.

The Journey

Let me begin by stating that I am not a psychiatrist or a clinical expert. I am simply a woman who has experienced and survived the phases that you go through when Life Happens. For me, the reality of it occurred during my season of the Empty Nest. The Empty Nest Syndrome is REAL! Originally, I thought it was just another psychologically driven phrase that had been created to describe an unreal experience. How quickly I had to retract that train of thought.

Empty Nesting is a time of evolution. It is a time of reflection, redefinition, and exploration. It is only when you do these things that you can effectively maneuver your way through the maze of this time in your life. Contrary to popular belief, empty nesting is not something that just happens when all of the children have left home. Think about it, a nest is by definition "a structure or place made or chosen by a bird for laying eggs and sheltering its young".[7] Consider the first part of that definition - a structure or place made or chosen. Another definition is "a place of rest, retreat, or lodging".[7] Work is a place made or chosen. A relationship or marriage is a place made or chosen. Home is a place of rest, retreat, or lodging. People can be places of rest, retreat, or lodging. So, if we lose any of those by choice or by chance, we find ourselves with our nest becoming empty. The nest is not just our home, it's our hearts, our visions, and for some, our identities.

Being an avid reader, when I realized the feelings that I began to experience, my first thought was to research information. There were articles from psychological based organizations that discussed the symptoms and treatment of Empty Nest Syndrome. "Treatment," I thought, "I'm not sick!" Yet the reality is if you do not address the mental and emotional changes that take place during this time, you can begin to experience physical symptoms. You can become sick, withdrawn, and depressed.

My nest was empty for several reasons. Life happens, and when it does, those things will empty the nest within you. I had gotten a divorce. I had experienced a job layoff – twice in 3 years. I had turned 50. I was dealing with an aging parent. Ultimately, my nest was empty as the single parent of a soon to be college student and had to face the reality of that phase of my life.

During her junior year of high school, I tried to prepare myself for the time when she would leave home. I asked questions like "What will I do with myself?" "How will I spend my time?" Little did I know that these questions would only begin to scratch the surface of what my experience would be when that part of life happened when there was no one in the house but me.

There were two things that I knew. (1) I knew the day was coming and (2) I knew that I did not want to be one of those mothers that lived through the life of their child because they didn't have one. I thought about my surroundings. Not only the physical dwelling of where I lived, but also the neighborhood and those that I came in contact with on a daily basis.

At that time, I was living in the house that my ex-husband and I had lived in together. I had remained there after the divorce because I wanted to maintain some level of comfort and stability for my daughter. The reality of the matter was that I did not like living in that house. It was a reminder of a bad time of my life and it was a struggle. Part of that struggle was because 6 months after I got divorced, I was laid off from my job. Like most people I was not prepared for that to happen. So, during my daughter's senior year of high school, I made the decision to move out of the house and we moved into an apartment close to her high school. I felt a sense of freedom! I didn't have to worry about the lawn, trimming trees, replacing fences, or the dreaded Homeowner's Association!

I soon came to another realization that the time was *now* to determine the steps I needed to take to not only learn who I was, but in some ways to redefine who I wanted to be. Why? Because life would happen again in some shape, form, or fashion and I needed to be prepared.

> "The journey of a thousand miles, begins with a single step."
>
> ~ Lao Tzu

Roberta Bogany

The Empty Nest Syndrome?

"Be open to what comes next for you. You may be heading in one direction and then life brings you another that might be a good thing."
—Natalie Cane.

The Mayo Clinic describes the Empty Nest Syndrome as a "phenomenon"[8]. I took offense to this definition in that it made it seem that it was not something real. It also states that many persons who find themselves in this situation have an "identity crisis".[8] This crisis of identification of self is an accurate depiction of the fact that for many years, and as a parent it's usually 18 years, you have described yourself by what role that situation played in your life - wife, mother, employee, daughter, etc. Some of those titles will remain, but the level of involvement or what your role will be in that sense has changed, and therein lies the foundation of what creates the crisis. Yet, here's the thing, no matter what the reason for you finding yourself in that time of evolution, it is because life happened, and the important thing is to work your way through it. Consider it a new journey and don't be afraid of what you will find along the way.

What are the reasons that your nest is empty? How has life happened to you?

1. _____
2. _____
3. _____
4. _____
5. _____
6. _____
7. _____
8. _____
9. _____
10. _____

Now that you've determined the reasons that your own internal nest has become empty, let's begin to take the steps to refill that empty nest.

How to Reline Your Nest

During my journey, I discovered 10 things that helped me to reline my nest. I PROMISE you, if you work through these 10 things, you too, will find a new nest full of life. You may not need all 10 each time life happens, but if you touch on each one, you will know if you have to work through it or can move to the next item.

1. Grieve
2. Relax
3. Reclaim
4. Complete
5. Live/Plan
6. Create
7. List
8. Reconnect
9. Release/Renew/Expand
10. Celebrate!

Ready? Here is where the real work begins!

1. Grieve

"There is no grief like the grief that does not speak."
  - Henry Wordsworth

Grieve the Loss

Yes, Life Happens. The ending of anything in your life is a loss just as death is a loss. It is important to grieve the loss in order to move past it. The phrases "just get over it" and "let it go" are easy to say, but not necessarily easy to do for some. It's ok if you need some time to determine what that journey will look like for you. There is no definitive rule to determine the best way for you to grieve your loss. Try several and see what works. It may be a week, or for others it may be a month or years. I just caution you to be aware of anything that can become detrimental to you. Drugs, promiscuity, and overindulgence of anything is not the way. Be careful of isolating yourself from everyone and everything. If anger, cynicism, and depression are a part of your everyday existence, then you may need some professional help in dealing with this loss. THERE IS NO SHAME IN GETTING HELP! If your employer has an EAP program – USE IT! It is a free service to you and there will be nothing reported back to your employer about the utilization of services. If you are a believer and there is someone in your place of worship that you can talk to, DO IT!

One of the worst things that I did during this time was to turn away from who I am spiritually. It was not immediately evident that this was what I was doing, but in not grieving the loss or even acknowledging it, I placed the blame everywhere but where it should have been – and no, not everything was my fault. Yet, it was just as important to determine what part I played in each situation and own it. Those admissions were a big part of growth for me.

What I learned that works for me, is to first have what I call a "purging session". I take a day or an evening to think about the loss and why it IS a loss. I acknowledge what the loss means to me and sometimes I take some time to cry it out. Tears are a way of cleansing. There is a lot of truth in the phrase "have a good cry". Your good cry may include yelling, screaming, cursing, or gnashing of teeth, and that is ok. In an article by Psychology Today [9] on the positive effects of tears, it states that it is important to shed tears for you and what you are feeling, not for someone else. The article also reminds you that the right amount of time for you to cry is whatever amount you decide. There is no time guideline on shedding tears for your situation just as there is no definitive amount of time for grieving. It is important however, to be conscious of how long you grieve. If you find yourself feeling low longer than you thought you would, please consider talking to someone. It doesn't matter if that person is a friend, family member, or someone that you work with – the important thing is to NOT hold it in. Let your feelings out and talk it through. For some people, writing is a way of letting their feelings out. If you use it like a brainstorming session, and just record anything that comes to your mind, it can be very helpful.

Years after the sudden death of my father, I found myself in a deep depression. In many ways, I was a Daddy's girl and did not realize how his death had wounded me. Of course, there were other things that also played a part in the depression, but it was time to peel back the layers of pain and begin to heal.

Unbeknownst to my family, for a long time the sound of an ambulance siren would make me sad. Al-though mine was not a situation of where an ambulance had come for my father on the morning of his death, the sound of a siren for me, was symbolic of the finality of taking someone away never to return. During the time of this depression, I was working in Florida, so being away from all that was familiar to me and being alone compounded the feelings of sadness. I sought counseling, and one day the therapist asked me to write a letter to my father. I thought that this letter would just be a simple statement of how much I missed him. It was not. It was filled with anger and I kept saying how unfair it was for him to leave me and not say goodbye. It was the beginning of dealing with feelings of abandonment and rejection that I did not know were there.

It is important to determine the best way to purge your emotions and grieve your loss. Don't let anyone dictate what your process should look like for you. It is YOUR journey.

After you discover the best way for you, continue to use it each time there is change in your life. You will find that anytime you need to purge and move on, you will go back to that form of grieving the loss and you will have an easier time of letting go and moving forward.

"What we have once enjoyed deeply we can never lose. All that we love deeply becomes a part of us."

- Helen Keller

GRIEVE

Ask yourself the following questions and journal your thoughts.
1. What did I lose?
2. Why is it a loss?
3. How does this loss make me feel?

_____

_____

_____

_____

_____

_____

_____

_____

_____

Roberta Bogany

2. Relax

"You may not control all the events that happen to you, but you can decide not to be reduced by them."

- *Maya Angelou*

Give Yourself a Break!

As I'm sure you've already figured out, I love motivational quotes and sayings. They are quick little reminders of the positive and good things that I should bring to my life. One that I came across during the evolution was this:

> Realize that you are your own biggest critic. People do not see the faults in yourself that you do. So, realize that they are not faults, not imperfections. They make you, you. -Unknown

Here is another one:

> We have to learn to be our own best friends because we fall too easily into the trap of being our own worst enemies. - Roderick Thorp

I like the last one the best! Why is it so easy for us to believe the worst about ourselves but not others? Ladies, if someone pays you a compliment on what you are wearing, most of the time you will say "This old thing?" instead of just saying "Thank you" and recognizing that you are looking cute. Gentlemen, the primary reason that you will NOT ask for directions is because you don't want anyone to know that you are lost and have no clue where you are going! (Guess what, we still know!) We spend more time agonizing over something instead of facing the reality, finality, or whatever other "ity" we should face. I had to tell myself the following:

1. Ok, you got laid off. While it may be hard to comprehend and things may be tough for a minute, you really will be ok! (And you didn't like that job anyway!)
2. Unfortunately, divorce happens every day – and because all things work together for good, it may be a blessing in disguise!
3. You didn't know? 50 is the new 30! You are wiser, stronger, and ready to really start living! IT IS ABOUT YOU!
4. I know she is your baby, and you are going to miss her. Just remember that going to college doesn't mean they are removed from the family! (And they will still ask for money!)

Give yourself a break! I've made my share of mistakes throughout my life! Life happens and we are not perfect! If we were, think how boring life would be? Look back over your life to this point and see how far you have already come and applaud that!

If you are a person who is supportive and provide words of optimism for others – do that for yourself.

Give yourself a break by acknowledging that it is what it is. Scarlett O'Hara in Gone with the Wind[10] was the perfect example of giving herself a break. No matter the situation, whether the Yankees were coming, Tara was burning to the ground, or when Rhett Butler had walked out on her, her response was "I'll think about it tomorrow, after all tomorrow is another day."[3] And it is. Allow yourself a chance to breathe. Don't spend all of your time thinking about it. You can relax. In the words of a wise therapist, "Wait and see."

"Relax and be free. You don't have to prove anything."

— Marty Rubin

RELAX

What are some ways that you can give yourself a break and relax?

_____

_____

_____

_____

_____

_____

_____

_____

_____

_____

3. Reclaim

"At 50, I began to know who I was. It was like waking up to myself."

- *Maya Angelou*

Reclaim a lost interest

When I turned 50, I didn't begin to take inventory of all of the things that were missing, I took inventory of the things I wanted to do. I made a list that I called "50 at 50". It was a list of 50 things that I wanted to do during my 50th year of life. Not all of them were things. Some of them were thought processes. The first item on my list was "face the fear". It was easier to say "the fear" than to list all of the fears that I had.

One of the things that I had always wanted to do was to get a tattoo. I can't explain why, I just did. Up to that point I had not gotten one because I was afraid of what people were going to say. See, I was the good girl – the church girl – the one that always did the right thing. I had fallen into the wave of thought about what kind of people got tattoos, and it was all a bunch of baloney. Getting a tattoo was NOT going to make me a bad person. I just thought it did.

So, on the day I turned 50, I faced the fear of what people were going to think about me and I got a tattoo.

Once I faced that fear, I started to examine the reasons I was hesitant to do other things and most of the time it had nothing to do with me, but my anxiety and insecurities about what others would think. I thought about the things that I used to do that brought me joy and wondered why I had stopped doing those things. Soon after, I saw the following on a plaque:

> *We don't stop playing because we grow old; we grow old because we stop playing.*
>
> *- George Bernard Shaw*

What a true statement! Many of the things that we truly enjoy we stop doing because we have "grown up". Was it a craft? Reading? A game? Writing? Playing a sport? Go back and reclaim those things that brought you joy! You may not enjoy them anymore, but you may also find that you do.

"We're very lucky to be able to go back and reclaim something that was a very special part of all our lives."
    -Roger Andrew Taylor

Reclaim a lost interest

What are some of the things that you <u>used</u> to do that you really enjoyed?

1. _____
2. _____
3. _____
4. _____
5. _____
6. _____
7. _____
8. _____
9. _____
10._____

4. Complete

"It does not matter how slowly you go as long as you do not stop."

- Confucius

Complete unfinished projects

If you're anything like me there are at least 5 unfinished projects around your house. For me that number may be close to 20, then add another 50 for the myriad of scrapbooking pages and albums that I have yet to finish. My daughter's Sweet 16 party, her high school graduation, prom, dropping her off at college, the girls' getaway trip, my first time traveling alone – so many unfinished projects. What is it that is unfinished for you? I remember saying "I'm going to finish those" – and now here we are 2, 5, 10, 15 years later and I have dusted, moved, and reorganized them many times, but I have NOT completed them. So, NOW is the time! Don't overdo it and set yourself up for failure, start small. Maybe it would help to only bring out something that you KNOW you can easily complete. This will give you the confidence to move on to the next project. Make it a party – invite some friends over that like to do the same thing or maybe they can help.

The important thing is to start – and keep going! If it helps, set aside a specific day/time to work on a project. If you determine that it is something that you no longer want to do, get rid of it! That's still progress!

"Rest if you must, but you must not quit!"
   ~ Rudyard Kipling

Complete an unfinished project

Which projects are you going to finish first?

1. _____
2. _____
3. _____
4. _____
5. _____
6. _____
7. _____
8. _____
9. _____
10. _____

"A dream written down with a date becomes a goal.

A goal broken down into steps becomes a plan.

A plan backed by action makes your dreams come true."

― *Greg Reid*

5. Live/Plan

"There is so much more, still worth fighting for"
- *Brian Courtney Wilson*

Live For Today and Plan for the Future

So now we come to the decision of what we want to do today and in the future. Who do we want to be? What is it that you've always wanted to do? Why haven't you completed it? A degree? A certification? Specific training for taking that hobby to the next level? Redecorating the house? Downsizing? Complete relocation? This is your chance to make some things happen!

I vividly recall a moment after my daughter first went away to college. I went to the grocery store and for a few minutes I just stood in the aisle. I didn't know what to buy! I didn't have to load up with frozen pizzas snacks, hot chips, sodas, and yogurt – and I didn't know what to buy FOR ME. I didn't know what amounts I needed FOR ME. My life had been filled with making decisions for her and designing/scheduling things that would be good for her and I do not regret a moment of it! But now – it was time for me.

On my drive in to work one morning as I sat in traffic, I thought about the commute. On a good day it was an hour and 15 minutes. If you know anything about traffic in Houston, there were not many good days, so at a minimum, my drive in was an hour and a half. On this particular day, it took me 2 hours to get to work – 2 hours!! I knew then that in order to have a better quality of life, I needed to reduce my commute time. That would mean moving – and fear set in. I had already moved from a house to an apartment, but this was different. It would mean moving to another part of the city. I had lived on the North side of Houston most of my life, so where would I go? How would I feel safe in an unknown area? What about my family? My friends? My church? Being the person that I am, I made a list of what it was that I was afraid of. Here is what that list looked like:

1. I won't be close to my family
2. I won't be close to my friends
3. I will have to change churches
4. I'm just scared

I looked at that list and wasn't sure what to do. Later that same day, after having a talk with God, I countered that with a response to each of the things on the list.

1. *I won't be close to my family* - They don't visit you now.
2. *I won't be close to my friends* - You might need new friends.
3. *I will have to change churches* - A new church may grow you spiritually and socially.

4. *I am just scared* - God did not give you the spirit of fear.

It was that last statement that did it for me. The fear went away, and I began to look for a new place to live – on the other side of town closer to work. I made the move and have loved the area that I now live in!

Start to think about what you want your life to look like – today and tomorrow. Don't limit it to things, also include thought processes and relationships. Are you spending time with friends? Do you need new friends? Have you become very cynical in your thoughts because of a failed marriage, job, and/or friendship? What do you want? No really, WHAT do YOU want? Ask yourself that question and try brainstorming by writing down everything that comes to your mind for a 5-minute time frame. You will be surprised at the items you have suppressed that are still there. There are some things there that will jumpstart you into determining what your next steps will be for today and for the future.

"There's only us. There's only this. Forget regret—or life is yours to miss. No other road. No other way. No day but today" ~ *from RENT*

Live/Plan

What do you want to do?
    Who do you want to be?
        Where do you want to live?
            What does your ideal life look like?

_____

_____

_____

_____

_____

_____

_____

6. Make a List

"Before you eat the elephant, make sure you know what parts you want to eat."

— *Todd Stocker*

Write an "I want to" list and do it!

Don't dismiss the power in making a list! It is said that "a list helps you discern and progress with a clearer, lighter head."[9] Take that brainstorming session that helped you to see what you want and make a list of those things. If it is what you want, and it's legal to get/do it, then you don't need any- one's permission to make it happen. Writing things down for me was good because it provided a place that I could revisit what I had said or my thoughts. When I'm "in the moment" a lot of things go through my head that I don't readily remember. Your notes area on your phone is a good place to capture them. Even doing a voice recording while you are driving is a good tool. I have come to love the One Note application that is a part of the Microsoft Suite.

My list looked like this:

I Want To:
1. Travel
2. Eat Healthier
3. Create or reconnect with friends
4. Let love into my life
5. Declutter
6. Get Financially Savvy
7. Celebrate ME

I started to see a recurring theme in the things I wanted to see happen in my life. Just know that there are some bold steps you will have to make in some aspects to make those things happen. I didn't realize that in order to reach the goal of traveling, I would have to learn to be comfortable traveling alone. This meant that I had to learn to be comfortable with ME! I didn't know that I had hidden behind some insecurities with the mask of not wanting to do things alone. The first trip taking my daughter to college, I couldn't find anyone to go with me, so I was forced to do it alone. Imagine my surprise when the trip back was spent not in tears but reflection and joy! I had broken through the fear of it and embraced what it had brought to me! That made the next journey, traveling to Miami, an easier one. I wanted to go, was able to go, but had no one to go with me. It didn't stop me, and I had a great time!

Make your list, set the plan, and make it happen!

"Write the vision; make it plain on tablets..."
Habakkuk 2:2

Make a List

I Want To…

1. _____
2. _____
3. _____
4. _____
5. _____
6. _____
7. _____
8. _____
9. _____
10. _____

7. Create

Where there is no vision, there is no hope.
- *George Washington Carver*

Make a vision board

There has been a lot of things written over the past few years about vision boards. The concept isn't new, but they have become very popular. A vision board is "a tool used to help clarify, concentrate and maintain focus on a specific life goal."[11] For some, they post pictures on their refrigerator. For others, they post words and/or pictures on their bathroom mirror. For me, it was a poster board. I made an event out of it and the first Christmas holiday that my daughter came home from college, we both did vision boards. We had such a great time going through the magazines that I had saved specifically for this project and even more important was the conversations that we had about our goals and why they were important to us. She could see the strides I was making to grow, and I could see how even in the few months she had been on the college campus, she was changing.

I took my vision board very seriously and placed it in a location where I would see it daily, if not multiple times a day. I would ask myself what were the steps I was taking to make those visions happen. "What am I going to work on today" was a frequently asked question.

Vision boards will give you a visual reminder of the things you want to accomplish. It's easy to say that you want a better life, but what does that life look like? This is where the vision board helps.

"Vision is the art of seeing what is invisible to others."
- Jonathan Swift

Vision Board

What pictures/items will go on your vision board?

_____
_____
_____
_____
_____
_____
_____
_____
_____
_____
_____
_____

8. Reconnect

"We cannot start over, but we can begin now and make a new ending"

-Zig Ziglar

Reconnect Spiritually and Relationally

Life happens. It happens to all of us. We get busy and forget about, put aside, or completely stop some of the things that we should do. So now you can move forward in reconnecting with people and things that you have cast aside to do Life – and begin life anew.

For me, it was relationally and spiritually. At first, I did not acknowledge my part in the demise of those things. I simply put the blame on others. My level of expectation was that they, and in this instance, "they" were my family and friends, should be the ones to reach out and make sure I was included in things. What I came to realize is that over the years they had become accustomed to the distance *I* had created, and it was up to me to make my presence known again so it could be missed when I wasn't around. Once I took responsibility for that, it became easier for us to connect, relearn, and better understand each other as siblings, friends, and individuals.

One of the things that happens to couples before the empty nest is that they don't spend as much time with each other. So now that the nest is empty, there is an opportunity to reconnect with your significant other. "An intentional time of rediscovery should be enjoyed in which a couple not only rediscovers themselves but also rediscovers one another." [12]

Another area of reconnection for me was my spiritual life. The fact that I was a believer had not diminished, but the amount of time I spent in prayer and just the simple act of reading a morning devotional had been lessened and, in some ways, removed. I also had been a little angry with God about how some things in my life had turned out. I should have known that he was shaping, molding, and preparing me for the things that would be a part of my future.

As a part of the move, I made to another part of the city, I reconnected with a church I had attended many years ago and instantly knew that this was where I needed to be and that the best was yet to come. My spiritual connection has grown, my faith increased, and I've seen God do things in my life that leave me speechless. All I had to do was make the effort. He was waiting.

Reconnect

What or who do you need to reconnect to?

1._____

2._____

3._____

4._____

5._____

6._____

7._____

8._____

9._____

10._____

9. Release/Renew /Expand

"Surrender to what is, let go of what was, have faith in what will be"

- Sonia Ricotti

Release or renew friendships, make new friends, and/or expand your social circle

In some situations, you simply have to realize that there are some friendships that you are better off without. Do not be sorry to lose those. Maybe they served their purpose during that time and that is fine, but you are not the same person, and this is a different season in your life. There have been some instances for me where I tried to renew an old friendship and found that we just didn't have anything in common anymore. While I was sad, I was not going to go back to being who I was at that point in my life. I didn't make an issue of it, I just let it go and buried it. I realized that I needed to make some new friends and, in some ways, expand my social circle.

Be careful here, because you can easily be pulled into an aspect of who you *think* you should be as opposed to clarifying who you really are and acting on that.

One example was after my divorce I felt that I just didn't have "it" anymore. I felt rejected, abandoned, and unattractive. Social media became my friend. I met people through that source and thought that in order for me to become a new person, I had to adopt the behaviors of some of those people. When I look back over that time in my life, it is hard to believe that I was that person. I did some things that I am not proud of. Nothing illegal, but things that were outside of who I am. I met some great people, but also met some people whose conversations included statements of "you should" or "this is how you" and I quickly latched on to that. I was wounded. I was hurt. I was lonely. I was lost – and all of those things made me an easy target. The people and places that I thought would be there for me were not, so I clung to those that were. Yet deep within me was that still small voice, that kept saying "You don't want to do that" and "that's not who you are". The more I listened to that voice, the more I began to pull away from those behaviors and I am so thankful that I listened.

My point here is not to say how evil social media is, because the reality is that it is the people on social media that drive whatever behavior that is displayed. It's no different than if I wrote profane words on a sheet of paper and gave it to someone. We can't blame the pen and paper company. I was the one that held the pen and wrote those words. Stop blaming social media for exposing who YOU are. The ownership is on you.

The big moment of change for me was in attending a workshop for women held at the church I attended at that time. The person who spoke gave me clear insight into where I was and what I needed to do to begin to come out of the fog that I was in. I then began to connect with people who were on a similar journey. People who I could learn from and grow with. I also began to connect with people that allowed me to grow in a social way. Through a dance class. That gave me many new adventures and joys.

When you start to do things that you truly enjoy and become the person that you are meant to be, you will draw those to you who are destined to be there and live the life that you desire.

"Our deepest fear is not that we are inadequate. Our deepest fear is that we are powerful beyond measure."
   - Marianne Williamson

Release/Renew /Expand

What people do you need to release?
What friendships should you renew?
Where/how do you want to expand socially?

_____

_____

_____

_____

_____

_____

_____

10. Celebrate

"Who am I to be brilliant, gorgeous, talented, fabulous? Actually, who are you not to be?"
- *Marianne Williamson*

Celebrate you every day!

I am as sentimental and sappy as they come, and I love holidays! It's probably not a surprise to you that one of the best days of the year for me is my birthday. I look forward to it and through the years I've given myself several parties. I used to do it because I was afraid that if I didn't give myself one, no one else would. Now I do something special on that day to celebrate me simply because I love me. More importantly I've learned to not wait until that day but do something, every day to celebrate ME! It's never outlandish or anything that would hurt someone else by doing it. It's never with the intent to make anyone else feel bad or to express conceit, it's simply a toast to the fact that today was another day that I was given. I am grateful and that is my way of honoring that. Sometimes I just sit with a cup of herbal tea in the evening and enjoy some good music. Sometimes I watch one of my favorite old movie musicals that I've seen 175 times already but sit there like I've never seen it before. Sometimes I treat myself to a good meal or my favorite dessert. Sometimes it's thinking of what craft project I'm going to do next. Many, many, many times, it's just thinking of something positive that happened to me that day, acknowledging something I learned, or reminding myself of what I am working towards. I celebrate the fact that in spite of everything, life happened, and I am able to continue forward, to grow, and become better.

"One of the wonderful things about Oprah: She teaches you to keep on stepping."
  - Maya Angelou

Celebrate You Everyday

What are some ways you can celebrate you?

_____

_____

_____

_____

_____

_____

_____

_____

_____

_____

My Nest Runneth Over

"There is something you must always remember, you are braver than you believe, stronger than you seem, and smarter than you think"
- *Winnie the Pooh*

Michael Strahan, the former NFL player now "all-over-everywhere-on-TV" man, wrote a book called "Wake Up Happy"[13], and while I can't honestly say that I do that (not a morning person), I can say that I do ask myself the question he posed in his book of "How can I get to happy today"? At first, I felt very strange doing things for me just because I wanted to. I was accustomed to putting my daughter first or work first or family first or whatever the need was at that particular time. Now I'm sure that I have some family members that would say that everything used to be all about me, and in a sense they are correct. You see, when you haven't properly gone through the process of grieving the loss, giving yourself a break by not placing the fault of everything on your shoulders, and the other steps in cleansing and preparing yourself for this next season in your life, you think that the loss in your life is because life is against you or it's everyone else's fault, that you are not lovable, that you are a failure, and "I'm the one that no one thinks about!" I was the Pity Party Queen and no matter what words of wisdom were provided to me, my response was "Yes, but...."

There was a time that I did not watch Oprah on TV. I did not DVR her show to view at a later time and always used the excuse that I was working as to the reason why I did not see it. Then during her final season, I started to watch the show – and I enjoyed it! I learned things and could tell I had some work on me to do. I asked myself, "Self, why didn't you watch her show before?" and in a true "Aha moment", [14] I had to emotionally strip myself naked and acknowledge that it was because I was jealous. I was jealous that she was doing something that I know I would enjoy and do well. I was jealous of her success – not materially, but her success at being Oprah. I could tell in watching her that if no one else acknowledged her or gave her another accolade, it wouldn't matter because she was happy being who she is and being HOW she is.

I began to look at the things that I had done during my life in order to align myself with what someone else had determined I should be. Clothing, hair, jobs, relationships – it was all so that I could keep up and not feel left out – and guess what, I was STILL left out. I had become so afraid of life that I had convinced myself not to live it. Yet now, it was ok. It was ok now because I was with the best person that I could ever spend my time with – me. I have really learned to love and appreciate who I am and the strengths and gifts that God had blessed me with. I have learned to love my time with me and if I decide I want to do something different besides be with me, I can. A good friend of mine used to tell me that I gave people too much power, and it took me a long time to understand what she meant by that.

During the process of relining my internal nest, I discovered what that meant. It meant that when I celebrate me, I don't have to depend on anyone else to do it. If they want to join me in the celebration, that's great, but I don't need them in order to have a parade. A funny thing started to happen when I had that awakening, I started to draw more positive people to me and the time I spent at home alone was because I chose to be – not because I had no other option. That doesn't mean that I don't have my moments, of course I do, but they don't paralyze me. When the next loss happens – and it will because life happens, I know what steps to take to get through it, so my nest is never empty.

"When you stop learning, you stop growing, and when you stop growing - you stop living" Roberta

READING RESOURCES

Here are just a few of the titles that helped me along my journey over the past few years...

30 Days to Overcoming Emotional Strongholds – Tony Evans
Complex PTSD: From Surviving to Thriving – Pete Walker
Called, Appointed, and Anointed – Janny Grein
Embracing Excellence – Carolyn Tatem
Identity – TD Jakes
In The Meantime – Iyanla Vanzant
So Long Insecurity – Beth Moore
The Charles Stanley Life Principles Bible
The Gifts of Imperfection – Brene' Brown
Wake Up Happy – Michael Strahan

Just for Fun:

Beverly Jenkins – I love all of her books!
Molly Harper – The southern titles (Gimme Some Sugar, etc.)
Diane Moody – The Teacup Novellas
Janice Hanna Thompson – Lots of good ones!
Pat G'orge Walker – The Sister Betty books are a HOOT!
....and too many others to mention!

REFERENCES

1. Holy Bible: New American Standard Bible (NASB).
2. Disclaimer definition – www.websterdictionary.com
3. Commissioned. "Love Isn't Love". *Go Tell Somebody*. Light Records. 1986. Track 2.
4. Adrozzo, A. 1945. If I Can Help Somebody. [Sheet Music]. Boosey & Hawks, Ltd, London.
5. Reprinted with permission from Haynes, T. "Live As If You Have Arrived". 2009. Personal Post.
6. Bignon, J. "On The Other Side of Through". *On The Other Side of Through*. Atlanta International. 1998. Track 2.
7. Nest definition - http:www.yourdictionary.com/.
8. Empty Nest Syndrome – http:www.mayoclinic.org/healthy-lifestyle/adult-health/indepth/empty-nest-syndrome/art-20047165.
9. Psychology Today – https://www.psychologytoday.com.
10. *Gone with the Wind*. Dir. Victor Fleming. Perf. Vivien Leigh, Clark Gable, Hattie McDaniel, and Olivia de Havilland. Metro-Goldwyn Mayer, 1939. Film.
11. Vision Board – http://makeavisionboard.com/what-is-a-vision-board/.
12. Kevin. A Thompson – http://www.kevinathompson.com/empty-nest.
13. Strahan, M. 2015, "Wake Up Happy", Simon & Schuster, New York
14. Aha Moment definition – http:www.merriam-webster.com.

JOURNALING PAGES

The following pages are simply for you to use to journal as you please. It could be thoughts, feelings, ideas (write the vision), accomplishments or even frustrations.

www.ingramcontent.com/pod-product-compliance
Lightning Source LLC
Chambersburg PA
CBHW021410290426
44108CB00010B/470